GW00685654

Attitude

TO CHANGE YOUR LIFE –
CHANGE YOUR ATTITUDE

Rosie Hamilton-McGinty

A WINNING ATTITUDE

Summersdale Publishers Ltd
46 West Street
Chichester
PO19 1RP
UK

www.summersdale.com

A Winning Attitude Program
www.awinningattitude.com

E-mail: info@awinningattitude.com

ISBN 1 84024 404 6

Printed and bound in Great Britain.

To my two sons Andy and Matt
who have been 'the light of my life'.

Introduction

The Code of Emotional Literacy

The basis of one's character is self-discipline, the virtuous life – based on self-control. Strength of character is being able to motivate and guide oneself, whether in doing work, finishing a job or getting up in the morning. We need to be in control of ourselves, our appetites, our passions and to do right by others. It takes WILL to keep emotion under the control of reason. Being able to put aside one's self-centred focus and impulses has social benefits: It opens the way to empathy, to real listening, to taking another person's perspective. Empathy leads to caring and compassion. Seeing things from another's perspective breeds tolerance and acceptance. In this sense emotional literacy goes hand in hand with education for character, for moral development and citizenship.

Develop Good Character Ethics

Character ethics:
A set of moral principals –
a personal code of right
conduct. Always do what is
morally and ethically
correct, it keeps your
conscious clear.

Enthusiasm

A positive attitude
attracts others –
always demonstrate
enthusiasm in whatever
you say and do.

Pride

When you
respect yourself
others will respect you.
Take pride in your
individuality.

Honesty

Be trustworthy.
Start by being honest
with yourself.

Fidelity

Faithfulness and loyalty.
Build solid foundations in
your relationships through
good communication.
Learn to share your
problems.

Courage

Ability to control or
suppress fear.
Turn fear into faith
and go forward.

Integrity

Honesty and wholeness.
Develop a character
based on love and
compassion. Integrity
cannot be purchased;
develop it now.

Modesty

Unpretentious.
Develop self-confidence
and drop the ego.
Be proud of
who you are.

Humility

Manners – humble attitude of mind. Develop courtesy and modesty in your dealings with others.

Justice

Fairness – exercise authority.
Trust that justice goes
with truth.

Industry

Diligence – business activity.
The more effort you
put into your work the
more rewards you reap.

Simplicity

The fact or quality
of something simple.
Go back to basic living.

Intuition

Listen to your intuition.
Trust yourself and
your perceptions.
Have faith and confidence
in what you feel.

Happiness

When you get up in the morning you have two choices: to be happy or unhappy. The happiness habit is developed simply by practising 'happy thinking'.

Forgiveness

Forgive – but learn
from the experience.

Trust

You can only trust
others when you
fully trust yourself.

Wealth

When you have
good health, you
have great wealth!

Anger

Feelings of extreme displeasure. Develop willpower to control negative emotional feelings.

Envy

Jealousy and
discontent with
what one has.
Don't envy anyone
– wish them well.

Greed

Excessive desire
for food or wealth.
Develop self-discipline
and self-control,
find a balance.

Lust

Intense desire
for something
– usually short lived.
Learn to balance
your desires with
other interests.

Laziness

Develop motivation
and a positive attitude.
Help yourself – by
developing your
talents and skills.

Boost Your Self-esteem

Self-esteem is how you see yourself as a person. If you value the type of person you are, you have good self-esteem – you are proud to be you. People with good self-esteem respect others as well as themselves.

Good self-esteem:
feeling good about yourself
enables you to be the
person you want to be
and enjoy others more
fully – offer more of
yourself to the world.

Low self-esteem can create a vicious cycle – lack of self confidence, unhappy personal life, poor performance, distorted view of self and others. People with low self-esteem put themselves down, fear failure, take the easy way out, resist change. Learn to be responsible and make necessary changes.

Make light of criticism – it stems from insecurity.

If a situation is beyond
reconciliation, distance
yourself to regain your
self-esteem.

Whatever your level of self-esteem, take positive steps to improve it. Start by being honest with yourself. Develop a positive attitude by giving yourself: Acceptance – recognise strengths and weaknesses. Encouragement – take an 'I can do it' attitude. Praise – take pride in your achievements. Trust – do what makes you feel happy and fulfilled. Respect – be proud of who you are. You can improve your self-esteem, it's really worth the effort.

I have valuable
skills and talents.
I respect my intelligence.
I act on my feelings
and beliefs.
I like my appearance.
I am worth knowing.
Basically
– I like who I am.

Develop A Positive Mental Attitude

Your attitude is important because it's the state of mind in which you approach a situation. It is the same you – the only difference is your attitude, which only YOU can control.

It's not enough to know the difference between a good and bad attitude, you've got to put your knowledge into action. It's up to you – you're the one who determines your attitude – in the way you look, what you say and the way you behave.

When you arise say out loud:
'I believe this is going to be a
wonderful day. I believe I can
successfully handle all the
problems that will arise. I feel
good – physically ... mentally
... emotionally.'
If you repeat these phrases
and meditate on them you
can change the character of
your day by starting off with a
positive frame of mind.

Your attitude will improve
when you act the part of a
happy confident person –
laugh, sing and smile.
Do this for five minutes
every day.

Enthusiasm, energy and determination are essential ingredients to progress. Set goals – give yourself something to aim for. Set your sights high – but be realistic.

Success is the next step
– past failure.

Your attitude affects how you feel physically and mentally and affects how successful you are in achieving your goals.

Your attitude should always
be the same whoever you
are with – always be
positive and helpful.

A positive attitude always wins the day. What you give out will return to you multiplied.

Negative Thoughts

The feeling of confidence
you have depends on the
type of thoughts which
habitually occupy your
mind. If you constantly fix
your mind on negative
events that might happen –
you will constantly feel
insecure and unhappy.
As you think –
so shall you be.

Positive Thoughts

Confidence and happiness
are what you want, flash
out all your old worn out
thoughts and fill your mind
with fresh new creative ones
– of faith, love and
goodness.

Positive attitudes are developed – start developing yours today.

Take Pride
In Who You Are

When you are looking for
success and happiness, you
must believe in yourself
and have faith in your
own abilities.

For a life which is full of joy
and achievement, you must
have confidence in your
own powers.

The way you behave
is a reflection of
your character.

Smile

A friendly smile gets everyone off to a good start – be cheerful even though you may not feel like it. Have a sense of humour – don't take yourself too seriously, sometimes a little humour can put everything in perspective.

Learn to depend on yourself
that doesn't mean being
selfish, it means taking
responsibility for yourself.

Most of our unhappiness
keeps us living in the past
and prevents us fully living
in the present.

Never take counsel of your fears, they can create stress and unhappiness.

Praise yourself when
you deserve it,
be kind to yourself.

Learn to address
and deal with what
makes you stressful.
Take time out to
reflect on necessary
changes.

Trust yourself and
your perceptions
– have confidence
in your abilities.

Learn to listen to
your inner voice
– it will guide you.

Learn To Welcome Changes

Experiment with new ideas, be flexible. Cultivate a sense of humour.

Don't take life
so seriously – have fun.

Take time out to
reflect on where
you want your life
to go, then make
it happen – with
the right attitude.

You must close
doors before you
can open new ones.

Don't opt out
when things
become tough,
it's never too late
to make changes.

Learn to accept and enjoy responsibility. Commitment has its rewards.

Change your life
by changing the
way you think.

You're the one with
the power to
change your life
– start now.

Winners
And
Losers

– Which One
Are You?

Characteristics
of Winners: they have
a presence, charisma,
enthusiasm; they look
and feel confident; they
are always well turned
out; and they have a
positive attitude.

Remember, your attitude to a problem determines the end result. Whatever you do success depends on your attitude. A positive attitude always wins.

Learn about
independence.
A true winner
depends on
his own power.

Tenacity: winners
succeed when
the going gets tough.

Winners have *oomph*!
They have
'get up and go'.

To be successful you must be a winner and be positive. Qualifications are a bonus. Winners take special care of others by providing outstanding personal service.
Take time to consider others; this attitude marks a true winner.

The secret of good relations
is to adopt the same attitude
with everyone you meet:
a winning attitude.

The first step
to a winning
attitude starts
with you.

Share Yourself With Others

Bring love and light to others. It not only brightens their day but also yours.

Share problems by communicating – a problem shared is the first step to resolving it.

Take time to be
with others and
to share thoughts
– relaxation
is heaven sent.

Make a mental
note to praise
when someone
deserves it.

Make someone
happy every day.

Be thoughtful
in your actions,
it costs you nothing.

Learn something from others by listening and be sincerely interested in them – in their point of view.

Think before you act.
A few moments'
thought can save
embarrassment.

Learn to cooperate
with others to achieve
common goals.

A positive attitude is infectious. Spend time with people who feel good about themselves. Self-esteem affects your attitude.

Learn to distance yourself from negative thinking people – their presence will affect your performance.

Be dependable –
dependability is
important to
efficiency and
success in your life.

Charm your way to
success – the most
successful people
are charming.

Learn to treat
people with respect,
no matter what the problem
or situation. Show people
that you respect them
– everyone wants
and deserves respect.

Treating others with respect can make getting things done easier and more pleasant for everyone.

Positive Traits
Courtesy – Kindness
– Tenderness – Love.

Negative Traits
Discourtesy – Unkindness
– Cruelty – Hate.

Learn to develop love
and understanding
for those around you
– you don't have
to agree with them,
you just have to try to
understand them.

Show you care,
it can make
someone feel special.

Give something
of yourself,
even if it's just a
compliment
– it will make
someone feel happy.

Value others' opinions,
one is not always right.

Try not to be dogmatic
in your approach,
no one likes a bully!

Learn to be of
service to others,
take time out
to help them.

Take the initiative
to help – many hands
make light work.

Do not criticise others,
no one likes criticism
– everyone needs attention,
admiration and affection
... in large doses!

When someone
appears angry
with you send
them love.

Show others how
the right attitude
can change their lives.

Man thrives when
he feels that
he is successful
in being there
for others.

Be Courteous

Courtesy is good manners. Courteous people are polite, interested, understanding, helpful, pleasant and sincere.

Courtesy begins with a positive attitude. Thinking positively is the first step to creating more in your life – and getting more out of it. Believe in yourself, recognise your strengths and abilities.

To be courteous means following the golden rule. Treat others the way you would like to be treated yourself. You will find that most people will return your courtesy and respect.

Take time to help others be successful, one day someone will help you.

Courtesy is
consideration for
others – what you
say and do:
'Please'
'Thank you'
'May I?'
'Do you mind?'

Courtesy is good
manners and
makes you
feel GOOD.

Courtesy means being punctual in keeping time and dates. No one likes to be kept waiting. Being punctual shows consideration for other people.

Courtesy means
being sincerely
interested in the other
person – courtesy costs
nothing, but is
worth everything:
'How are you?'
'How is your family?'

Courtesy means be patient
and listen to the other
person even if you are not
particularly interested.
Communicate clearly so that
others understand you –
and be sincere.
It is easy to be sincere in
what you say and do.

Listen carefully to others. Courtesy means good communication – develop the habit of keeping each other informed of where you are and what you are doing.

You can develop serenity and quiet attitudes through your conversation. The words we use and the tone in which we use them – we can talk ourselves into being nervous, highly strung and upset. We can also achieve quiet reactions. Talk peacefully to be peaceful.

Being pleasant
doesn't cost anything
– it just makes
you more friends.

Success is about
being courteous,
thoughtful and caring.
Try it!

If and when people ignore
you, send them love and
always be pleasant.

'Sorry'.
A word that
breaks down barriers.

Start practising courtesy –
you'll find it pays
instant dividends, gives you
ease and poise, prevents
friction with others, speeds
action towards your goals
and makes you FEEL
GOOD!

Balance Your Life

Recreation. Enjoy yourself – plan leisure time, set aside time for personal recreation. Take time to find out what is and what's not important in your life.

Make time for hobbies.
All the great people
in life have hobbies.

Take responsibility
to create new interests.

He Who Plants Kindness Gathers Love

Always remember: what you give out – money, love or service – always comes back multiplied, but not necessarily from the same source that it was given to.

What goes around
comes around
– what you sow,
so shall you reap.

Give the world
the best you have
and the best will
come back to you.

The only safe
and sure way
to destroy an
enemy is to make
them your friend.

Take responsibility
for your actions.

Try reflecting on the following verse:

When there's righteousness in the heart
There's beauty in the character
When there's beauty in the character
There's harmony in the home
When there's harmony in the home
There's order in the nation
When there's order in each nation
There's PEACE in the world

Chinese Proverb

A little about Rosie
and her vision

I feel my role this lifetime is to assist
in developing self-belief within
individuals, encouraging them to take
personal responsibility to create a
happier, successful and more fulfilling
life.

The 'A Winning Attitude Program' has
been designed to help both individuals
and groups develop themselves, through
self-awareness. The program, which
includes Presentations, One-to-One
Self-Awareness Consultations and On-
site Therapy Relaxation Techniques

with trained therapists, helps to identify one's strengths and weaknesses and allows the opportunity for change and growth in both one's personal and professional life.

I am currently undertaking a Masters degree at the University of Brighton in Change Management. My aim is to link my background of personal development and emotional intelligence and take spirituality into organisations.

A Winning Attitude Program
www.awinningattitude.com

E-mail: info@awinningattitude.com